MATERIAL GOODS

MATERIAL GOODS

by
Janet Burroway

For Earlette —

"In a leap more
flight than fleeing..."

All best,

[signature]
Tallahassee
28 Feb '98

A Florida State University Book

UNIVERSITY PRESSES OF FLORIDA
Tallahassee

Printed in the United States of America

Library of Congress Cataloging in Publication Data

Burroway, Janet.
  Material goods.

  "A Florida State University Book"

  I. Title.
PS3552.U76M3   811'.54   80-12381
ISBN 0-8130-0670-8

University Presses of Florida, the agency of the State of Florida's
university system for the publication of scholarly and creative works,
operates under policies adopted by the Board of Regents. It's offices
are located at 15 Northwest 15th Street, Gainesville, Florida 32603.

Acknowledgments

Thanks are due the following publications for permission to reprint poems that originally appeared in their pages:

"Song" is reprinted by permission from *The Atlantic Monthly,* © 1957 by Janet Burroway.

The following poems originally appeared in *Granta*: "The Scientist," *"D'Accord,"* "Footnote," "Aubade," "James's Park" (under the title "Benevolence"), "Epithalamion," and "Introduction."

"A Few Particulars" was first published in *Twenty-Seven Poems,* University of Sussex Press, 1966.

"Lièvre aux Capres" is reprinted by permission of the editors of *Cafe at St. Marks,* © 1975, Apalachee Poetry Center.

"Hole" originally appeared in *Sun Dog,* © 1979 by *Sun Dog,*, reprinted by permission of the editors.

"Piecework" is reprinted by permission of the editors of *Delta.*

"An Affinity with the Garbage" originally appeared in *The Tallahassee Democrat* under the title "Shirley Church Has an Affinity with the Garbage," © 1977 by *The Tallahassee Democrat.*

"Lines to King's Cross Terminal" was first published by *The Critical Quarterly.* Reprinted by permission of the editor.

The following poems first appeared in *But to the Season,* Keele University Press: "From a Dry Doorway," "Proverb," "On Being Accused of Tame and Regular Verse," © 1961 by Janet Burroway.

New Statesman originally published "Nuns at Birth" (© 1970 by New Statesman) and "Separation" (© 1975 by New Statesman).

"Owed to Dickens" is reprinted by permission of Ballantine Books from the volume *New Poems by American Poets* 2, ed. Rolfe Humphries, © 1957 by Ballantine Books.

Several of these poems have also appeared in, or been produced by, *MS. Magazine, Borestone Mountain Poetry Awards, The Guinness Book of Poetry, New Poems: A P. E. N. Anthology, Universities Poetry* (Keele University Press), *The Yale Review, Sound and Sense* (ed. Laurence Perrine), and the BBC Third Programme.

For

Jessie June Burroway
Gladys Burroway
Michael Burroway
Elizabeth Humphries

aunt, stepmother, sister-in-law,
mother-in-law; four good friends

Contents

3 – Dividends

1 — Balanced Books

LAST REQUEST

Dear Reader, I have no complaint,
As long as you peruse my verse,
Concerning what you are or ain't,
Or your supposed ancestral taint,
Or whether you have gout or worse.
If only you enjoy my work
I will not press my luck too far:
Let skeletons in closets lurk,
And leave the door, if you like, ajar,
Or go and join the D. A. R.
Your wealth, I. Q., disturb me not,
But this I think entirely fitting;
My only plea, compatriot——
Don't read a lot of me at one sitting.

       For I the ultimate Ogden-lover,
       I the incurable fan of Nash,
       Sat down one day on an impulse rash
       And spent six hours behind the cover
       Of a vast anthology, to discover
       The plight of the turtle, the blight of the bore,
       The seven religions of Marmaduke Moore,
       "Reflections on Ice-Breaking"—quite a store
       That some librarian, I suspect,
       Had had the misfortune to collect.
       And I arose, as you might expect,
       A good deal sadder and somewhat wiser,
       A grave, incurable derelict,
       The ultimate Ogden Nash despiser.

While we're gay and young and fast,
Hunt my stuff in the daily locals;
And with the help of your bifocals
Look for me when youth is past
In publications of Condé-Nast.
Read my every iambic scribble;
Read my books, if ever I write one.
I promise you many a tender nibble
And never a serious, deep, or trite one.
None of the "moonlit" "sun-washed" tripe;
I'll serve you as well as I can in rhyme.
But promise me now while the time is ripe,
Before I even begin to type,
That you'll read my poems
One
At
A
Time.

> For I had discovered a bard named Parker,
> And read as the night grew dark and darker,
> Pausing only to put the light on
> (Leaving my finger as a marker);
> I was the victim she set her blight on,
> Hers was the volume I spent the night on,
> I was the sight that the bright sun rose on,
> Trying to read and put my clothes on,
> Starting "Big Blonde" as I pulled my hose on,
> Buried in "Tombstones" trying to walk,
> Turning the pages she put her prose on,
> "Here We Are" as I punched the clock.
> And if by night I was worn and swarthy,
> At least I'd had my fill of Dor'thy.

And if, in the year 2002,
You find my name (unknown to you),
By some good grace of the Lord above,
Ensconced in literature's "Who's Who";
Or Viking sells, at the price you love,
The volume marked, *Complete Works of . . .*
Contribute there your seven-fifty
(Go to the library if you're thrifty);
If you crave my verse, don't fight it:
Take up the delicate morsel, bite it,
If you've an impulse to, recite it;
That is the poet's fondest dream.
But read my poetry as I write it . . .
With

Intervals

In

Between.

THE SCIENTIST

"There's nothing mysterious about the skull."
He may have been suspicious of my request,
That being mainly a poet, I mainly guessed
There might be an esoteric chance to cull

Some succulent, unfamiliar word; that being
Mainly a woman, I now for his sake embraced
An object I held in fact in some distaste.
But he complied, his slender fingers freeing

(There must be a surgeon somewhere with stubby hands)
The latch that held a coil across "The suture
Between the parietals and occipital feature."
And gently, his flesh on the bone disturbed the bands

Which illustrated the way that "The mandible
Articulates with the temple next to the ear.
The nasal bone gives onto the maxilla here."
He laughed, "It's a bore, but it's not expendable;

"The features depend, if not for their shape, on the narrow
Cranium, formed of the commonest elements;
Weighing nine ounces, worth about fourteen cents;
Not even room for what you would call a marrow."

In words resembling these, he judged them dull—
The specimen, his detail, and my suggestion.
"The skin and the brain, of course, are another question,"
He said again, "but there's nothing to the skull."

And that must be so. The quick mind most demands a
Miracle in the covering or the core.
What lies between is shallow and functional fare:
My hand between this thought and the posturing stanza.

But his face belied us both. As he spoke, his own
Eyes rhymed depth from the sockets of that example;
His jawline articulated with the temple
Over the words, and his fingers along the bone

Revealed his god in the praying of their plying.
So that, wonderfully, I justify his doubt;
Am moved, as woman to love, as poet to write,
By the mystery and the function of his denying.

DREAM CALL

Can't recognize the voice.
It is either scared rabbit
Or dark Brer Hare,
My stripling self
Or the jungle lush,
Cunning, calling,
"Is April the right time?"

It must be cottontail,
Acute protestant,
Meek, whining
"April is cruelest."
It must mean:
The right time to tire, to cross
Over and try
Some other life, opt
Out, dye
The everlasting eggs, lie
In the resurrected grass

Since, this end of the wire, I rise
Black, my muscles bangled golden,
Scattering rodents in the undergrowth
With the wrath and jangle of my
"No!"

And wake, here.

KEEP OFF THE GRASS

Here they've stuck some steel rods in the ground,
Twisted at the level of my ass,
And looped a length of slack rope in between.
To save the grass.

This young stud comes by in his scungy cutoffs,
Solar plexus flexing in the sun,
And with a flippant wrist lifts out the rope loop
From every one.

I'm not impressed. It's only his profession—
Anti-authority, freedom, all that crap.
He's "stoned? " On "grass? " He kicks a little stone up
Toward my lap,

Flips me the finger, leers and shuffles past.
I'm happy to report that that is that.
I mean, what if it was me the bastard lifted,
Me he tilted at,

What if he laid me in the cracking grass,
What if the sun broke through,
And the stones broke under my back, what would I do?
I don't know what I'd do.

The point is, I'm a protector, by profession.
I'm on the side of rope and twist and slack.
I pass back along the stone path he's abandoned
And loop it back.

HAMFOOT

I tread heavily, have done so since I walked.
The floorboards are old, and if I hit them wrong
This cat will leave the rug in one wide arc
Over the sill, and land precisely poised
On the narrow slats of the fire escape outside.
I am not given to whisper. If I so much
As hum, he will start and stretch to the nearest sofa.
He is not fooled of how I feel. If my fingers
Are clumsy at his ears, they are not unkind.
Nevertheless I break glasses, so when I rise
He seeks the shelter farthest from my chair.

Listening to your footsteps, and the latch
That never has been fixed since the morning I
Twisted the knob too hard, I will lid my eyes
And greet you with a nod, turning a page,
Or focusing tightly on the needle's eye,
Anxious, alarmed, that you might start and shy
At the close encounter of such heavy love.

SONG

With whomsoever I share the spring
    I share my mouth,
And credit to him all birth, all south,
    All seasoning,

Who flies with the first bland breath of May
    To my chill bed.
Then whatsoever the vows I've said
    And will yet say,

There is no stirring of truth in me
    But to the season.
I tell you this that you may work treason
    On perjury,

And whomsoever you find untrue
Imprison to spend all springs with you.

MENDING

For a short while
I was all of a whole. These tendons
Gloved my muscles slippery as sex
And I had a blinding stride.
My mind machined me.

Not spring or summer,
Nothing to do with seasons.
Oh, love, the cure-all, yes,
But what's effect?
I caused unions among bees
In November.

Well it is over.
My teeth are stitched together
In strange sentences, patchwork.
My kidneys, I believe, are making do.
Something in the stomach is unglued.
I taste the glue.

Make do a while, mend,
Sit still in the pine droppings
And wait for an ordinary cure, a season.
A shattered bone is still not entropy.
Sitting still will piece it
Till the season
Wraps around again.

D'ACCORD

It was not a matter of communication.
Rarely have two been so articulate,
Or so read between lines left themselves unread;

So the one would say, with effective hesitation,
"*War and Peace* . . . is a brief book. But I date
All tediousness from Wilde." By this he implied

A remark they both remembered in addition,
That Tolstoi "had no style, but could create."
Also, that he considered all art dead

Which lived by its skin. And as well his inclination
To paradox, as the straightforward way to state.
Which the other shared, who nodded and replied,

"Little things mean . . . a little, as only a Russian
And a Greek philosopher will quite admit."
Whereby was inferred a respect for daily bread

And the bitterness of his Aunt's repatriation;
Also political views of a liberal heat,
Which were none of them things the first would have denied

So that nothing went in need of explanation,
Or need for us, except for the mutual hate
Which both of them, always, innocently hid.

FOOTNOTE

Except for Darwin, they advise:
    "Find for yourself a humble seat,
    And sit cross-legged at their feet
Who feast at banquets of the wise."

I have done so. And of the scraps
    Collected, not the least are these:
    Wystan Auden has narrow knees,
And cotton stockings that collapse

Around his ankles. When he talks
    He slips his loafers off and shows
    Yarn-yellow patterns—and his toes—
Through frayed holes in the argyle socks.

(It wouldn't do if I had said,
    "Sir, so profound is my respect
    That, if you will, I will erect
My monument in darning thread.")

Marianne Moore wears saddle shoes
    In suede as soft as velveteen,
    Like college girls. But hers are clean.
(Oh, it is not my place to choose

To say politely, "Marianne Moore,
    Our minds are in accord, for I
    Have shoes like that. Perhaps we buy
Our books, too, at the same bookstore.")

Darwin, at least, observed that we
    Are able best to contemplate
    Standing on shoulders of the great.
(It doesn't help. *Les beaux-esprits*

Would count it all the more my sin
    On Eliot's shoulders to be seen
    Saying, "I know just what you mean—
My, how your hair is growing thin!")

A FEW PARTICULARS

Let me give an example of what I mean:
I think the dead aren't always the departed.
Isn't there something about worms? I've never chopped one,
But—awful!—a chicken dancing without its *head!*

That's relevant. How was it the Ancients put it?
Don't count your chickens until you're in the grave.
Believe me, whoever figured that one out
Had got the word from a mother on motherly love.

I'll be specific. The younger generation.
They say that Socrates had the same idea,
But I don't think that disproves it. Because decline,
For instance, can spread to the dogs they're going to.

And the fact is: dog eat dog. Why, that's in the blood.
If you hate who loves who you love, that'd be the reverse
Of logic, wouldn't you think? But just read Freud
and Francis Boas. They call it science. Of course,

I'm only speaking generally when I mention
My son has married the most, oh, dreadful woman.

EVEN COWGIRLS GET DEFENSIVE
(For My Father)

In my father's house are many mansions;
He weeds them out when the drawers get full.
We wrap the garbage in discarded blueprints,
We line the catbox with the plumbing specs,
I cut my baby teeth on a senile T-square.

His floors and roofs are flat, one story only,
The colors flat and brittle as rock-candy.
What can I tell you? —you who have never known
Such arid harbors, nor so bright a brown.
Bad painters only retire to my desert home,
Those who use their colors straight from the tube:
Red-orange, red, red-violet, violent orange.

"*Ô ciel!*" you exclaim at this description,
Whose heaven retires at tea-time in a dimity
Nightie gone gray from having been hung indoors.
But heaven at home sweeps stakes,
Throws the die poker-hot on Camelback
Mountain, and deals down my dad's enamels.
Would it be more tasteful if I say, for you:
"*Chez moi, alors, le soleil se couche en nu*"?

TWO FOUND POEMS

(Note: the lines in these poems have been re-arranged, but all of them come verbatim from the interviews identified.)

I. TOM SNYDER INTERVIEWS THE SUPERSTAR

Let's say you weren't Elton John
like a budgerigar in a cage.
I grew up,
I was a tea boy when I was going,
it was in '73.
My parents wanted me
to learn the piano,
sing in the choir.
I wasn't too keen.
I'm only 29,
loving and free.
If you forget the words—
I do forget the words—
loving and free . . .
Pause for these announcements.

Let's say you weren't Elton John,
the non-event of the year.
I was terrified as a kid;
I was born in Yorkshire;
my dad came home once a year.
At that time everything was, it was
very fashionable, cute and kinky—
black leather—
my dad came home once a year.
When I think back

I was discouraged,
I was very tired.
I don't know if that has any value.
Be funky, get down;
I'm not laughing.
I'll turn off the tape recorder now if you want.

Let's say you weren't Elton John,
an interesting phenomenon
whispering: I'm a chicken.
I wanted to do a duet;
that's an important step.
We couldn't afford the Carnie,
so we got the Albert.
I thought it would be a nice thing to do,
it was tongue in cheek,
very commercial,
get up offa that thing.
No way. We scrubbed it.
No way.
When you're onstage you feel dreadful
for a couple of days
twenty years from now
and we have to break.
We have to break.
We have to do these messages.

II. DICK CAVETT AND COMPANY SAVE OUR ELOQUENCE

How bad is our language, and
who's to blame?
Dick Cavett, John Simon,
John Kenneth Galbraith and Agnes de Mille,

hosting a show that was later aired
like you like it, just by accident
(some special training is required),
identify some of the culprits.
Government, civil service, the academic world,
grade school, high school on the lower level,
professors on the upper (even Harvard),
mathematicians, music, books,
the realms of art, the realms of culture:
it's perfectly all right.

Clarity of thinking is linked with
clarity of thinking—
a simple declarative sentence.
Who are the villains?
It simply isn't quite so simple.
What it is is a variety of rules,
those standards and regulations,
structural linguistics;
the point being is:
the scientific community,
the corporate bureaucracy,
the born aristocracy,
the plutocracy of the imagination,
the field of education,
Arthur Burns, the state senate,
psychiatric influence and the military,
people who were socially quite superior,
Tom and I,
Latin,
a bunch of snobs.

Shall we call it corruption,
the same kind of fastidiousness you get

from good dress, a higher good usage ratio?
Specific offenders, please.
We are in a deeper standby posture:
genteelism, spiritual elegance,
aggressive elitism, knee-jerk liberalism.
Now Howard Cosell, one of the sporting people,
I think that he believes the way he speaks—
"The mist drifted over the stadium
like a description in a Hardy novel"—
they don't know what you're talking about.
We don't want to be those characters ourselves,
myself, my wife and I,
Tony Ollasowitz.
If you abide by the rules people know where they are.
Security apparatus.

Slang is admirable.
Any group of people, juicy, racy,
those who have been deprived,
have to speak dreadfully or not at all.
Your sources are right.
Associate with the masses—real good—
any old moron, a pig, the other fellow.
Ordinary people grow up
without hearing the language—
a misconception of democracy—
cameras, television reports, reporters,
Channel 13, deaf ears.
A really good piece of slang,
the great tool, endowed with the equipment—
a string of words and then a dash—
oh man, like I says, far out.

But who's to blame?
Identify some of the culprits.

Imperfect thought, policemen, baseball players,
clowns, miners,
the everyday man who drives a cab,
Ed's way of life,
Haitians, Philippinos, and Chicanos—
the buggers, those people are unusual—
that part of the boondocks,
that part of the sticks,
the mass garbage (even Harvard),
John Kenneth Galbraith,
John Simon, Arthur Burns,
Dick Cavett, Tony Ollasowitz,
Agnes de Mille,
Howard Cosell,
Tom and I,
myself, my wife and I,
parents,
your life,
ideas,
the English language.

THE GARDEN OF EARTHLY DELIGHTS

In this garden of delight
Everything, my touch makes grow.
Belly-moss my fingers mow
Sprouts behind to finger height.
Rocks beneath the mosses grow
In this garden of delight.

Good. I have come to it of my own accord.
We will not choose packets in the A & P,
Share out the mowing and the mower repair,
Sweat over the location of the apple tree,
Take snapshots of the children in the apple tree,
Nor pile the compost where the spuds are stored.

In this garden, at my touch,
Juices run in every hollow.
Branches bud for every swallow,
Eyelids yield such sap that such
Flowing everywhere must follow
In this garden at my touch.

Good. Very good. My gardens always died.
I was fond of saying that my thumb was black
And I couldn't keep a houseplant in the house.
Shatter the potted roots. I will give back
The prickly pear to the desert. I will give back
The fig trees to the South. They always died.

In this garden of my power
I am rain and soil and sun.
At my touch the juices run,

The sprout unpetals hour by hour,
Liquid light is wrung and spun
In this garden of my power.

Good, good, good, good. Grow and harden.
This is the furrow I have wanted dug.
I have known roots and roots and only roots,
And now I want the flowers in my trug.
We will not deal with weed or worm or slug.
We will have harvest. I will have this garden.

LIÈVRE AUX CAPRES
(For John F. Kennedy — Ghent, 1965)

I think about *Macbeth* while I cook hare.
It isn't so much the quantity and the color
As a way it has of running in the cracks
And setting the fingerprints in high relief.
It alarms a middleclass woman to have fingerprints.

Now we have been properly outraged and thank God
If we're guilty for all those Jews we aren't for this.
The hare, who hadn't time to mind his dying,
Would have found my caper sauce indigestible.
Over coffee, we still discuss the assassination.

On the twenty-third of November the butcher's wife
Was gutting a hare and weeping into the mess.
She said, in Flemish, "Oh, Madame, it must be much worse
For you," and gestured with the bloody backbone
And burst real water from her eyes, no dry sob,

And I, all raw and runny, thought, astonished,
Well, no, it isn't, well, no, it clearly isn't,
Which represents more blood than I would have dreamed.
This tells well, over coffee. I do not mention
That she also soiled my glove when she gave me change.

They say sometimes one comes into a camp of men
As if deliberately. His eyes catch light like the barrels.
But there is no superstition touching this.
Strictly speaking, a hare is not a king.
Small game, and so they aim for the brain and take him

In a leap more flight than fleeing. I have never seen
One run, properly, live. Only in pictures.
And, let us be clear on this, I could never shoot one.
What I do know how to do is to use the blood
In cream, with mushrooms, capers and tarragon.

Delicious. Although we do not like his brothers.

2 – Liabilities

AUBADE

Hair, fleece, fur, shock above the skull,
       Hawk's down, falling sparrow's
Feathers; whatever intricately will
       Shelter minds and marrows

Is numbered just in the mind of God,
       They said. And it amounted
To a tame warning. I understood:
       Some things could not be counted.

Star. Star. Star. Star. And starlight braids
       Swung to the starlit world:
Uncounted over unkempt clouds
       The shining orbits curled,

And shrieking pigaback at stars
       I fingered through the brown
Infinity of my father's hairs.
       Undoubting, I sprung down,

Flung myself to the bearded shade,
       Whispered to the whiskered mass,
Nuzzled it; did not know the blade
       Inherent in the grass.

Hair, fleece, fur. Shocking *I* am bound
       To watch the sparrow mount on

Molting wings, and fall. I understand:
      Some things you cannot count on.

Grizzled fringe about the pate
      My fingers shrink to touch
I have the skill now to compute
      And it is not much.

The sky dimming to a gray dawn
      Has a few stars yet to yield.
The bald things twist and burrow in
      The mud of the shaven field.

HOLE

A woman is all orifice and vessel;
You may believe it.
I have mouths at all extremities.
My ears have throats.
My hands are hungry,
Muscles gulp in the arches of my foot,
My anus chews.

Nothing will fill me;
I have eaten monuments.
Books I digest to pulp.
Men will not do it—
Look at all these bones!
I suck whom I suckle,
I swallow their houses whole.

You should have reckoned on the force of
Gravity
When you dug this hollow.

CEREMONY OF INNOCENCE

There are seventy-three varieties of parrot,
Brilliant in plumage, popular in this zoo.
They do not fly. They are chained, most dignified,
To plaster branches, haughtily accepting
Popcorn out of human vending slots.

Being grounded is like blindness to a bird:
The other muscles take the part of senses.
Their feet mince coldly toward the tether's reach;
They are flaming in color, frozen in the eye.
Birds walk with ceremony who can't fly.

PIECE WORK

For all of it, she knew what she was about
With the down; for all of the spite
Spent in the piecing, needle-fierce-fingered,
Needle-eyed-piercing, scrappy, angered
Beyond belief at interruption or thread-knot—
She knew what puzzling business she was about
To clip, tack, pink, tie, whipstitch, to defray
Her heat in the painstaking, and it may be
That she somehow salvaged warmth enough in her quilt
To blanket her bare days' heart-shortfalling fault.

And he knew how dabs must mass to a careful line,
What stringing of dull Sundays went into *La Grand
Jatte*—needle-keen-seen, needle-brush-thrust—
He learned how mind at best is a *pointilliste*
Salvaging harsh lights from an unmixed palette,
Which, canvas confronted, daubs, stains, strains to fill it,
And having illumined what it could, will hurtle
To hope that some light makes and is made immortal.
Not that he might have bettered that petty lady,
Nor her skill delayed the blind young chill of his body.

Warmth, light; obscure mother, cold master;
How, once knowing the soul a frail imposter,
Patched, painted, spread in spite, in pride hung,
To make my fraudpiece at least some ordered thing?
I am all stone sown upon cold fallow;

All froth-fill sunk to a bare hollow,
All, all as a fall pavement, leaf-effort strewn,
And the crisp colors trod with the litter down
In the gutter, to decay and stain and filth.
How do I pattern the raveling of myself?

AN AFFINITY WITH THE GARBAGE

i adore you.
therefore
after i have got rid of the packaging
and the pits
after i have dug this gunge
out of the avocado pulp
and the pickle fork is boiled
after the parings
the seeds skin shells
crust skum and grounds are skimmed
after the handiwrap apple peel
and the waxpaper outer onion
and the brown card husk
are all disposed of
and spun away
after the bone
and the eyes and the core
and the raw inedible offal
are expunged
we will sit down to dinner.
and how was your day
in the real world,
darling?

INTEGRAL

This is the sense:
(It lends itself to prose
But needs to be clothed,
As you need to be in those
Indigestion dreams
Where you find yourself in shoes
And a G-string, singing blues
In the Methodist choir loft) . . .

That's half the sense.
And the other half is
Somebody's got your skin in
The tannin bath.
You stand stripped to the nerve,
Your sinews slightly shabby,
Your bones all out at elbow;
The Red Queen says, "I read in the *U. S. News* . . ."
A cheetah shrieks at your elbow,
Professor Channing mentions, "Juxtaposition . . ."
The Reverend Knott absolves, "My mother-in-law . . ."
And that is the very thing,
The very thing to untie your intestine.

The garbage of a single meal can drain me.
Across the quad is across, across, across.
In the aerial photography you may clearly see
The knees shatter as they knock,
The limbs dismember
Of their own discord,

Me frantic to avoid thee and flee,
Professor Cheetah, the children of Reverend Knott.

Except that I have stood
Barking, "Juxtapositional Mother-in-law!"
I have worn loden green.
I have blamed. I have blamed.
It was as long ago as Tuesday last
And dim in my flayed brain,
But I know I stood
Tapping my whip on the calf of my riding boot.

Lord, lest I take the easy stance,
Victim without tolerance,
Let me have occasion to be a brute.

JAMES'S PARK

A girl more beautiful than all her cousins
Trails praising plane trees for perennial valor;
Praises white roses for the face of pallor,
And deeper peonies for deeper reasons;

Thanks a rich urchin rigged up like a sailor
For setting forth the sailboat from his hand,
Likewise the blackbirds coming in to land,
Likewise the lover, governess, and scholar.

Time, ground, and gratitude she has to spend
On variant beauties of a day declining:
The sombre shadow and the silver lining,
The frail transplanted and the tangle pruned.

In warm appraisal all her view lies sunning,
And it is then unlikely she perceives,
Brushing her fragrant face in fragrant leaves,
How her all public radiance is thinning;

How she applauds herself among the groves
And blots the landscape with her little loves.

SHREW

Now that old love would wake and walk about the mind
Unshaven, shabbily dressed and out of sorts,
As after a troubled, interrupted sleep.
It got to the eyes, but not in a watery way:
They snapped, and her tongue trapped victims like a toad's.
And yet, from each according to his love
To each according to his luck, she had understood;
And that the debt lies with the one more loving.
She might have put that knowledge in new pockets
Had he not proven such a surly riser.
As it was, she spent herself in lullabyes
Like curses, and smiled furiously at strangers
Who passed with furtive glances at the ground,
Ashamed to witness such a stupid thing:
A full grown man who would not go to sleep.

MOONFUCK

Queene and huntresse, chaste and faire,
The module has entered your atmosphere.
The atmosphere on the color screen
Is of hyped avuncular anchor-man.
Who has just emitted a loud Hosannah
As, seated in his silver chaire,
Shepard has eaten a banana
And, heedless of the faulty coupling,
With the eloquence of Kipling,
Has sent this message from Diana:
"You guys look really great from here."

Goddess excellently bright,
They've sent Apollo, which isn't right,
But in the woods you ruled so grandly
A little incest was viewed kindly.
And why should heroes whose precocity
In measuring escape velocity
Has put our payload on the moon
Three years ahead of some Russian goon
Feel any impulse toward apology
If there are chinks in their mythology?

Young shepherds in Delos used to dream
Of catching in the dappled shade,
Or at her crystal-shining stream,
That fleet-foot huntress, yet a maid;
Each believing he could screw,
Goddess, excellently, you.
And what men dream about, they do

Sooner or later, though it's a fact
All systems go, and the final act
Is likely to have a different karma
Than what we get in the classic drama.

Now Uncle Wally's waxing madder:
Having ingested his banana,
Shepard is making for Diana.
The booted foot is on the ladder,
The silver glove is on the rung,
The thrill on Wally's silver tongue,
The Goddess shudders for her fate,
And Shepard says, "Boy, this is great! "
And divested, thus, of his poetry,
He is balling the moon with a golfing tee.

LINES TO KING'S CROSS TERMINAL
(For Eleanor Bron)

Across from me, a gentleman under thatch
Thick-trimmed against the weather at ear-high eaves
Sets his mouth ajar to admit his pipe,
Reproducing the outdoor mist, producing a wince
In the smoke-green eyes of the lady in the pince-nez.
It must be his wife between them. She shuffles through
A tattered Home Show shopping bag, and spades
Up the dry leaves of her adverts. On this side,
Beside me, a Cambridge undergrad going home
Plants noughts and crosses on the frontispiece
Of a Penguin, with a man in a pudding-bowl hat.

The East Anglian faces are mostly flat,
Their furrows plowed orderly downward, skirting the bumps.
What vegetable seeds of talk I fling
Fall into the ruckle, not affecting the look of the land.
As: "Isn't it cold for March. And dull for noon."
"More so than others," says the woman next to the man.
And: "That castle must be older than anything
Still standing in my home town." "You're not from here,"
The man with the pipe explains. They introduce themselves.
Their names are the Stoates, John Gallow and Lady Lindle.
The other, intent on rightly placing his nought,
Only tilts his brim down toward the seat
At the delta of green velour between his knees.
Above us over the wife's head and the boy's
Identical mirrors set in black wood frames
Exchange flat looks, and mirrors of mirrors of mirrors
Recede backwards into the length of the slowing train.

The process of coming to a halt takes time in England.
A muted screech, a minor lurch, a sign
Announcing, and then another, and then another
Announcing that this is one of a score of milk-stops
Before we achieve the King's Cross Terminal.

Lady Lindle, with a dull eye on her emerald,
Is making little hillocks of her hands,
Which gambol, rear, and romp upon the hide
Of an inverted black-dyed kid. How such
Cultivated ladies come to travel
Second class is no longer the subject of much
Discussion in England. In the green square of my window
The sheep abound. It is somewhat early for lambs,
But the ewes have cropped the fist-like hills as short
As my lady's late youth, no longer the subject of much
Discussion in England. I am doubly struck
By the emerald fallow lying left and right.

All halts are like this. Death succeeds decay,
And birth is happening in the silt most fallow.
False springs deceive the bud, and the fruit comes thin.
Lady Lindle shrugs off her tartan Mac;
Her belly rounds like the boll of a blighted tree.
We are off again among the luscious hills,
But she is tired, and will tire with every milk-stop
Before we achieve the King's Cross Terminal.

FROM A DRY DOORWAY

It was raining green the willow.
Weedy the asthmatic Pekinese,
Wheezing across the crabgrass, followed
After the flung and clanging piepan,
Pouncing it just at the rosehedge edge
Of that greenboarded and tintop thing
They called The Toolshed, where they kept the toys.
I hung one with the willow laughing
When, rainglutted, the drainpipe sloughed
The gutter water—Plang! —in the pan
And into and over his Peking cough;
Hung swinging one with the willow laughing
To Weedy, wet and piqued and peeking,
Claws mud-clotted, from the wetted hedge.
That was morning wonder and worldful
Up to the beck of a housedry voice
"Mercy! . . . This instant! . . . Catch your death!"
So he from the hedge and I from the willow
Scuffed and waded in at the door.
That was morning. But only one.
And I have wasted no wanting on
The dog dead, pan scrapped, rosehedge withered,
Willow uprooted rotting grey.
Only sometimes dry in the doorway
I have listened wist and witherful,
Chastened to hear my safened sound
Against the wet deathcatching weather;
Water and wishproof, and no longer
Having the sense to stay out in the rain.

LONG SHOT

I learned it like
the rest of my generation,
didn't I?
at the moment of need,
long shot of The Stranger;
dolly in;
close-up:
stars.

I have been panning,
haven't I?
panning
so much desert sand,
so much fool's gold,
so much celluloid
on the cutting floor.

Appears—
penultimate frame,
why not? —
too late for the plot,
The Stranger,
long shot;
zoom:
freeze frame.

LANDSCAPES

I

If it were, say, Satan loping among the rocks.
Everyone understands if a man sweats snakes
And scorpions breed in his armpits. You can get
Ahold of a forked tail, even if it's wet.

I mean that you do not lie. I don't mean you lie.
There is no dishonesty so lays me flat
As when you say what you mean, and my reply
Is a lie, and must be a lie, and another lie.

II

Really, there is a meadow in May light,
My son half-dazzled, your skin brown and bright,
And boys' things: how to build a castle, snare
A toad, tussling and tossing him in the air.

I mean, you are innocent. Please for all our sakes
Know that I know that you would not touch his hair
With the minutest harm, for all our sakes.
It is I who sit in the buttercups sweating snakes.

III

A wart-faced old man under an oak in the mist.
The wicked are those who will not share their crust
With his hunger. The pure in spirit do, from whence
The warts drop off, and the toad becomes a prince.

I can tell hunger. You are starving for a child.
Must I deliver out the dazzling prince?
Let toads be toads for once, and die in the wild.
I am famished too. I will not share this child.

SEPARATION

Maybe the woods aren't what they were. The mist
Purls in the sun rising on the butts and the empties.
The great foxhunt has left its radial wide-tracks,
A broken heel, a used rubber in a Sunbeam bag.

Still, some things are eternal. They still make traps
In the old style, rows of teeth on a steel trip-spring.
Spring! The teeth hit home in the fox's paw;
The fox still bleeds.

Maybe she doesn't know what she's getting into.
The instinct is as old as iron. She chews,
And doesn't realize till her own teeth try it
How hard it is to bite through a broken bone,
How tough a muscle is, the nausea
In a nostril bleeding backwards every breath.

Still, what would you have her do? Quit now?
The tendon under the center pad is severed.
Two toes are gone, and they're gone in any case.
The blood is under her haunches. The sun is up.

Maybe this argument is a lot too cunning
To offer to a row of teeth on a rusty hinge.

Still.

3 — Dividends

LINES ON A PIECE OF WALLPAPER

I have in hand a scrap of Gallagher's ceiling,
Rent from where its tattering cast the shade
That seems to be some grasp against a falling.

Since ten December, walls and the wee hours reeling
With echoes of all we had left not quite unsaid,
I have in hand a scrap of Gallagher's ceiling.

Here, so green too gentle a peace is hilling
The winter of Wales, no rise of a mist is made
That seems to be some grasp against a falling,

But fog like hearthsmoke where their hands are piling
Hills of unrealized diamond. Indeed,
I have in hand a scrap of Gallagher's ceiling

And oh, I could feed the green fog of goodwilling
And warm me down in the peace-decked hall of it, creed
That seems to be some grasp against a falling

When sheer excess of sweet is the season's failing.
But I am adorned in a warm unseasonal greed:
I have in hand a scrap of Gallagher's ceiling:
That seems to be some grasp against a falling.

PROVERB

It happened once, he waked the worm as late
As noon; scuffing a toe in sand too dry
For castles, he unearthed her small estate;

Found her, at least as impudent as shy,
The bait of fables, ringed around a root.
The worm turned in his mind some sort of why,

Since surely all the birds had fed. His foot
Replaced the sand-cocoon, but in his head
Proverbs were clearly open to dispute.

At nine, it's not a thing he would have said,
But his was logic lodging in a wink—
A profound purpose, not to be misled:

He owned no horses. Therefore to the brink
Of rivers no one else would ever know,
He led the lot of them, and made them drink!

He laughed, and counted but his poultry; oh,
Computing in less mathematic terms
His blessings, I suppose. At least it's so

The chickens all hatched. History confirms
He ate and kept his cake. And I profess
He owed it to the lethargy of worms.

That's all of it that matters. Nonetheless,
By some obscure 'in spite of' of his own,
He was the proverb quoted to excess;

The very Earl of Early, up alone
At dawn, surveying all his morning realm
And even catching, from his sandbox throne,

The songbirds, still asleep, up in an elm.

IN ANSWER TO A QUESTIONNAIRE
"What do you like, and why?"

"Put all things in their own peculiar place,
And know that Order is the greatest grace,"
My mother quoted, smoothing back her hair
And pinning fast the antimacassar where
My father's head would, with a sudden motion,
Sunder it anyway. She had a notion
To favor what was "Gentle," "Proper," "Nice,"
And, plumping pillows, practiced her advice.
For which example, if no other reason,
I am an advocate of things in season:
Of blessings counted, eggs left uncomputed,
Of constitutions gravely constituted.
I like my sky as blue as very sky,
My roses red as roses, and my pie
That easy, and with cheese; and in warm weather,
Small barefoot boys and girls in patent leather.
I like the taste of toothpaste, and the looks
Of carefully adjusted shelves of books
In perfect stair-steps, dusted not so much
By feathers as a browsing reader's touch;
And kitchen curtains white, with gingham border,
And budgets kept efficiently in order,
And odors chronologically consumed:
That is, my mornings shaving-cream perfumed
And bacon-smelling, and my afternoons
In wintergreen and starch and macaroons,
And Air-wick, Glass Wax, and adhesive tape,
Ink, chocolate, new paper, paint, and grape,
And evening reeking Lanvin and clean hair,
And ashes, and a T-bone, medium rare.

I like the mathematic, tidy sight
Of linear equations factored right,
And punks in poolrooms, praying for the seven,
The preacher in the church, and God in heaven.

"A sweet disorder in the dress is spice;
Variety and paradox are nice,"
My father improvised, and flicked an ash
On Mother's carpet, lowering a lash
And grinning dedication to his art—
"The whole may be as good as any part!"
And being tutored in the spice of life
By that philosopher, who loved his wife
As well as any other incongruity,
I am an advocate of ingenuity:
Of those who eat their cake and lick the fork
And make another cake; who love New York,
Who lead a horse to water, make him drink,
Defying sense, pour passion into ink,
And put it in an envelope and send it,
And win the girl; or get the check and spend it.
I like comedians I know are tragic,
And scientists who highly value magic,
And men of letters disregarding those
Poetic words they know to put in prose
Fresh fascination of the embryo.
I like still March, dry April, and Spring snow.
I know an actor out of work and poor
Whose name is Bouris, whom they call The Boor;
The close-shave refugee of seven marriages
Postponed because of opportune miscarriages.
Who loves the theatre and cannot act,
Whose character is caught within the fact

He's sloth itself, and Order's first offender,
And doesn't shave . . . because his skin is tender.
I like him. I like books where cripples walk
And any medium where objects talk,
And stern professors, therefore, who define
"Pathetic fallacy" and quote the line.
I like the thought that weddings need rehearsals
And love is found in radio commercials.
I like gay funerals. And I like the rumor
That there's Divine Wrath . . . Justice . . . Sense of Humor.

APPLEYARD ODYSSEY

I am racing the freight headlong by boxcars
To the dirt crossing at Appleyard. I have a need
Of distressing with the tip of my nose tonight
A moustache of ambiguous character,
Raffish and academic; combing to order
With the tip of my nose an ambiguous moustache.

Pitted against this nose and this moustache
Are society, several statutes, eighteen years
Of hard-earned sense; boxcars of impedimenta.
I recognize the risk of a wreck when I see one.
But I said need, and I will race trains for it.
I take headlong that heavy cargo.

The engineer mistakes me; I see him leaning.
He thinks when I hit forty in the dirt,
Signal darting the intended turn,
That I will take these odds. Careful of himself,
Careful for his cargo—for me, maybe—he leans
A long blast on the wail of the warning horn.
That prohibition cuts a skyward moan
They can hear as far north as the Georgia border,
South to the alligators at Wakulla,
Till it runs relief down when I brake and skid.

Purged as Odysseus by the heavy touch
Of the goddess' voice, I sit at the crossing,
Raffishly cognizant that the SPC
With a load of motor parts and cheddar cheese,

The Illinois Central hauling paperbacks,
And a two-ton South Coast Transport full of cornflakes
Are all, when you come down to it at the crossing,
That stand—and they are passing—between you and me.

OWED TO DICKENS

A chef whose hat is celluloid and green,
Whose pots are paste-pots, and whose spice is spleen,
Has cooked my goose. And even now is wooding
The stove to offer up December pudding
So lumped and limp no Scrooge would dare dispatch it
Toward the Christmas feast of any Crachet.
I can conjure visions of his doings:
Deadlines thudding due, and winter brewings
Steaming from the copy desk technician
Even as I scan the May edition.
No Chuzzlewits, Pips, Pockets, Pumblechooks
Invade his introverted pocketbooks,
But heroes grave, anemic and repressed,
And heroines perennially undressed;
Sex, sects and sin, seduction and sedition,
And prices slightly higher Denver West.

Oh, I'm a modern child. I'm overjoyed
With doses of cod liver oil and Freud.
But All the Year Round, modern publications
Grind to grounds my greatest expectations,
And psycho-pseudo-subtleties look quaint
By one brand of Victorian restraint.
Ah, label me a love-sick infidel,
But give me Tiny Tim and Little Nell,
A Magwitch and a Wopsle and a Wemmick,
With happy endings grandly epidemic,
Where Fagins fail, and Dorrits get their due;
Where Olivers and Orlicks *font la queue*
With Pickwicks clicking as the trick plot thickens,
And Dickens doling out the derring-do.

UNIONS

People may lie in a meadow, and they do,
truant from meetings of the A. A. U.
P. like me, like you delinquent with the I. T. U.
in favor of four skyscapes and a honeydew.
They can and do.

These unions protect our welfare. So let's posit
still another association of the elite:
The Amalgamated General Lotus Eat-
ers annual members' subscription fee is due.
Herewith, our deposit.

EN FACE
(For Robert Piccard)

Face me. And if I say I like your face
Better than any I have ever seen,
It's not facade or surface that I mean,
As if I were taking an option on a place,
Stating a preference for brick or wood,
Gable or hip, refurbished or decaying . . .
I am not buying houses, neither the buying
Nor the houses. And if I were, I should
Speak of the primal function of a door
As being to open outward, to invite,
And of windows that let in and spill forth light.
Look—if I like the way you look, it's more
As if to say, I like the way you see.
That when you face me, what you face, is me.

DOUBLE EXPOSURE

I am pretending to brush my hair
At the long mirror, with you as audience;
Bare-breasted and bare backsides; hence
Aware that you see both sides of me. Aware.

Aware of the filaments falling to my wingblade,
My arched brow, and my lashes; and the shocks
Of love-damp pubic hair and my scolding locks:
Active tresses in a lead I have never played.

I have known actress and actor
Who couldn't abide the Round.
The nape of a neck is bound
To feel noose-naked to an actor.

Even those who seek and cling
To public exposure like a mask,
If they are trained in the old ham-tragic task,
Find the Method menacing.

So I have never done exactly this,
Stood full-view pretending to brush my hair;
Of myself, the mirror, and the man aware,
Wearing my nudity like a consummate kiss.

But you may see me lock and stock and whole;
There is no crevice that I need conceal.
You, when you review my flaws, reveal
To both of us the complex human role.

So I may brush my hair, may play this part,
May stand in your sun spot while you look your fill,
May stand still. And you may circulate the still
And fix it in the promptbook of your heart.

EPITHALAMION

Child-eyed among the Brooklyn cousins,
Leanne *The bride wore cotton lace*
     caught at the hip
in a bow of peau de soie, and dozens
of pearls of sweat adorned her face
     at the upper lip.

She is Mrs. Souzis now. *The troth*
was plighted in Hawthorne, New Jer-
     sey at four o'clock
in the August afternoon. A Goth-
ic spire of straw and jersey shir-
     ring sheltered the shock

of a neighbor's gilded hair, and wear-
ing a tear-stained-glassy stare was
     the mother of
the groom, in a rawsilk bare-
back sheathe size twenty-two. The air was
     stale under cov-

er of orange blossom and pomp-
ous organ, and wilting toward the alter,
     the bride's bouquet
of asters and ivory swamp
azaleas went, in the damp, unfalter-
     ing fist of gay

Leanne. We left at last, adjourn-
ing in paper-draped coupés to where

Sherbet and champagne
were served at Schweisguth's on the Turn-
pike, decorated for the affair
    with cellophane

reception guests, exchanging brit-
tle titters through the rows of pink
    rosettes, and through
the jazz of a borrowed band. A skit-
tish bridesmaid drenched her skirt in drink,
    and impromptu

not too long after that, *"Old Man*
River" was rendered by Nelson Keeting,
    and a round of jokes
on sex and the single state began,
through which the bride sailed slowly, greeting
    the Brooklyn folks.

Oh, Leanne. Settle in Brooklyn. Raise
flower girls for export. I extoll
    whatever rites
are wronged, whatever heavy haze
of cheap cigar smoke sends the soul
    toward wedding nights,

seeing the simple way you thread-
ed silkenly among them; smiled,
    oh, wholly of
them, hallowing the day, your wed-
ding and their world with a pure, child-
eyed trust in love.

MARRIAGE VOWELS

(For the Freen)

A   nswers escape me in the main, although
E   very blessed moment I proceed as if
I   had them pat, insisting, idly strident, that
(O   nly God, or Goddess, or the gods, can know)
U   nder it all, it's up to us, and utterly enough.
Y   ou are my authority for testifying that it's so.

And sometimes, why.

NUNS AT BIRTH

This wing is quick with nuns. They flock and flutter,
Their habits whisper, sweeping the corridor.
The mildest human sound can make them scatter
With a sound like seed spilled on the immaculate floor.

They know about waste. They come with disinfectant,
Troubling the peonies bursting on my sill;
Their quick white hands can purge the most reluctant
Stain, and the sprouting germ, and the alien smell.

Old men have said—and my anxious, Baptist mother—
That purity is the fallow ground of love.
It is here in the sterile sheets and the smell of ether,
And their bead-bright eyes. But what are they thinking of?

Or that Superior Mother about her labours:
What discipline could inform so bland a nod
When I shrieked and he shrieked and the bursting fibers
Gave him up to her quick white hands in blood?

Or the dove-grey novice now in her sterile plumage,
Who will go about birth, and about it: his hot greed
And my thickly weeping breast—what sort of *homage*
Brings her white hand fluttering to that bead,

Because it is that, my love! Her breath has quickened
At the noise of his pleasure in the immaculate air
As if some glory sanctifies the fecund!
Well. Twenty centuries' lies are brought to bear

In her innocent misconception; the germ sprouting
In the cell, the chalk on the alien door, the hot
Salvation of witches, the profits and the prating—
We have not bought those lies. But we must have bought

Some lies. We are consumers, you and I.
And now this third, gums leech-fast at my breast,
Whom we shall wean to an epicure, and say:
Self-sacrifice is ingratitude, is waste;

And say: husk the kernel; feed at the fountains;
Seek sun in winter at the belly of the earth;
Go to the east for splendour, the north for mountains;
And always go to the nuns in time of birth.

ON BEING ACCUSED OF TAME AND REGULAR VERSE
(For Dudley Fitts)

Listen. Guts are fine and I have got them.
I know no greater order than is put
In motion in the making of my ordure.
No drumming heel of my poetic foot
Can render rhythms as my kidneys plot them.

O in my arteries there is an art!
Entrails distill the meat that my tongue sluices,
Meticulously, like a poet, picking
Whatever is impure and waste from juices
That veins, in perfect iambs, take to heart.

And yet my heart's another matter. What's
Impure, improbable, pied, mute or mutable
It stops at, and staccato at lace ferns,
Fauns, seas clichély deep and owls inscrutable,
Revolts against the symmetry of guts.

If it is tame convention that the rose
Will die in perfume over the green thorn
And the green thorn in other seasons wither,
I will be tame, conventional, and mourn
In meters of my bloodbeat all that goes.

But not my going. When my ordered bowels,
As ordered, yield precisely to my death,

Then stay my moulding with no icy fluids:
Embalm my veins with fernsap, young deer's breath,
The ocean's deep-most green, and the eyes of owls.

And let me in disorder decompose
To some new poet's tamely flaming rose.

MATERIAL GOODS

1. Still Life

Catching the burnish of the earthenware,
The apple core with the teeth defined,
Veins in a petal, duck down on the neck
Of a duck with a broken neck:

These have been thought
Not merely exercises for the brush,
Not etudes for the epic still to come,
But the thing itself, worth framing,
Unveiling, celebrating, worth hard cash.

They are not battle, they are not Jove in judgement.
But buildings have been built to house them, grey
Scholars and the yellow press have mourned
Their theft, their bombings, their decay.

Domestic things made minimally less mortal.
Still lifes. Still,
Life.

2. Domestic Help

I have lost touch with the vestal mystery.
It isn't me
Who finds the pine
Needles in the shag from last December's tree,

Vacuums up the pins and the threaded eye,
The buttons, the nailparings,
Doghair, traces of body ash;
It's not I but she
Who combs this mortgaged haystack,
Pitches the forks to their proper shelf
For little better than minimum wage.

We have passed the age
When it is myself
Who puts the boy in the bath,
Pares his nails, needles the dog;
It is he himself
Pitches bone at the pine,
Stacks the forks and the Decembers,
Shags his hair,
Buttons his mystery.

It is not me
Who vacuums up my dying dad,
Pitches the needles into his pared skin,
Nails him against the last December tree;
It isn't me
Who combs his hair against the mortgaged bone,
Shelves his ash, buttons his eye;
It's—who?—back home
Who wages touch
Against the proper minimum mystery.

I have bought time,
Paid minimum,
So that my pared eye

May trace this little better than
Minimum thread,
May bring home the loss,
May touch the mortgaged vestal mystery.

3. Middle Ground

Up over the canker in Iran,
Those bitter streets,
and a bad pecan
That has bit back
In the cavity we can't afford,
You pause as I pass
And offer me a smile
Phony as a poem.

Between mouth and mind,
The galled nutmeat on the immediate tongue
And the brain ranging
After the deposed kings and the bloody gutters,
Your mind makes room
For my intermediate riot of stirred air,
Your mouth makes room
To tap out the message
That it is all right, here.

Between us is middle ground.
Middle age, income, crisis;
We are merely middle dying.
What you do daily is re-Morse to me:
You send your face as phony as a poem.

As, for example: it is I who am reading the news;
I have the toothache; I look up and smile.
In the middle ground
Between the shriveled bitter and the riot
I write the poem out of your intent,
Where we may afford
Both smiles, which may both occur and mean,
That it is all right,
No more phony than a poem
Of the married kind,
Married, and kind.

INTRODUCTION

That was spring's going: fingers of stroking sun
Coaxing a crinkle into the water's face,
And a winking brighter than before, and bolder;

She with her knees confined in the loose embrace
Of arms still pale to the bare of shoulder,
Shy to the glance of sun on the summer dress;

He no more than half a season older
Ambling toward the lake, and a slow caress
Of his own left cheek with a pensive thumb;

Nothing so grand as fate, but nothing less
Than the fact that, searching hermitage, men come
Choosing mutual places of isolation.

Something—a shadow of spring's dissent, or some
Descending mist, at least, of hesitation—
Wrapped the surface in sudden rapt reserve,

And they, agreeing, remained in contemplation
Some ways apart, in no sort of love to serve
A human thirst, but drinking the scene together

Until the thin cloud splintered. He found the nerve,
Then, to predict the summer's coming. Whether
He meant the season alone he didn't say,

But she replied in polite words of the weather,
And yielded the chaste, proud profile to display
The full face waiting of a summer day.

Photo: Bill Humphries

Janet Burroway

About the Author

Janet Burroway was born in Tucson, Arizona, September 21, 1936. She was educated in Phoenix, Arizona, and at the University of Arizona, Barnard College (A.B. cum laude 1958), Cambridge University England (B.A. with First Class Honours, 1960; M.A., 1965) and the Yale School of Drama (RCA-NBC Fellow, 1960-61). She has taught at the University of the State of New York, Harpur College at Binghamton, the University of Sussex, England, and the University of Illinois, and is presently Professor of English at Florida State University, Tallahassee.

Her published works include five novels: *Descend Again* (Faber and Faber, 1960); *The Dancer from the Dance* (Faber, 1965; Little, Brown, 1967); *Eyes* (Faber, 1966; Little, Brown, 1966); *The Buzzards* (Little, Brown; 1969; Faber, 1970: nominated for the Pulitizer Prize, 1970); and *Raw Silk* (Little, Brown, 1977; Victor Gollancz, 1977; Pocket Books, 1979); two children's books, *The Truck on the Track* (Jonathan Cape, 1970; Bobbs-Merrill, 1971; Pan Paperbacks, 1972); *The Giant Jam Sandwich* (Cape, 1972; Houghton-Mifflin, 1973; Pan Paperbacks, 1975); one chapbook of poetry and one translation. She has recently completed a sixth novel, *Opening Nights,* and is at work on a textbook for fiction workshops.

Her poems and stories have appeared in *The Atlantic Monthly, Mademoiselle, New Statesman, MS., Story Quarterly,* and other magazines. She was awarded the AMOCO prize for excellence in teaching in 1974 and a National Endowment for the Arts Creative Writing Fellowship in 1976. In early 1980 she was Visiting Lecturer at the Writers' Workshop, University of Iowa.